Dare to Be Free

Dare to Be Free

How to Get Control of Your Time, Your Life, and Your Nursing Career

James Huffman, RN

Writers Club Press

San Jose New York Lincoln Shanghai

Dare To Be Free
How to Get Control of Your Time, Your Life, and Your Nursing Career

Published by Writers Club Press
an imprint of iUniverse.com, Inc.

For information address:
iUniverse.com, Inc.
620 North 48th Street
Suite 201
Lincoln, NE 68504-3467
www.iuniverse.com

ISBN: 0-595-09855-X

Printed in the United States of America

CONTENTS

Preface vii

Acknowledgements ix

Introduction: A Short Story about My Life 1

Dreaming: How Visualizing Your Future Will Change Your Life 5

What Are Your Dreams? (Your First Lifetime Question) 9

Evaluating Your Dreams: Where Will They Take You? 13

Evaluation: Putting Your Dreams into Reality 15

Evaluating Your Experience 21

Positioning Yourself for a Successful Career 27

Getting Business to Come to You 31

A Brief Word about Equipment: What You Need,
and What You Don't 33

Earning Your Living out of Your Home 37

Specialty Areas for Your Nursing Career 39

Nursing Business Ideas Requiring No Money (or Almost None) 43

Hospital Nursing and Other Areas 51

Sales and Nursing 61

A Little More Searching: the Internet and All That 65

Books & Other Resources 69

Here's Where It Ends 73

Index 75

PREFACE

Tuition is high in the school of hard knocks. This book (really a manual) is an attempt to help you avoid some of that high tuition! I have met many nurses who would like to be in business for themselves, but they can't figure out how to do it. What you are reading here will help you to be successful in business, in a business as a nurse, and as an entrepreneur.

Many more nurses are unhappy with what they are doing, or where their career is heading. This will be helpful to them as well. And in all situations, I encourage feedback and questions. If you have compliments, complaints, suggestions, or inquiries, send them to me. This is a manual, and not a book, so it can be updated frequently, as situations change. I am not some fount of wisdom, and I will happily change problems in the manual that are pointed out to me. Contacting me is easy. E-mail: huffmanjim@hotmail.com, or by fax at (336) 226-2767, or by mail at P. O. Box 2274, Burlington, NC 27216. If you write by mail, *please* include a self-addressed, stamped envelope. (And by the way, I *really like* hearing from my readers, and knowing what they are thinking, and hearing their suggestions).

I encourage nurses reading my manual to think for themselves, and not be afraid of trying new ideas. Don't always rely on "experts," and that includes me! However, I am also available for consultation with nurses who are planning out their careers. What I have found is that we often have blind spots, and are unable to see obvious skills and talents that we have. My consulting is reasonably priced. If you feel "stuck" and can't figure out where to go, my fees may save you thousands in career blind alleys. Write me for prices and details.

I am also available for speaking to your nurses association, alumni group, academic department or other such organization. Some of the topics I'm available to speak on are: "Getting Control of Your Life and Your Nursing Career;" "Visualizing Freedom in Your Nursing Career;" "Successful Nursing Practice in the 21st Century—Even When You Don't Have a Bachelors Degree;" and "Managing Your Time for a Happy and Successful Nursing Career." Other topics can be personalized for your group or convention. Contact me for free, no-obligation information.

And now, begin your journey. Life is not a final destination, but a journey of love and learning. Start today!

ACKNOWLEDGEMENTS

For those who have encouraged me along the way: for my wife, Amy, and my wonderful children, Matt, Katie, Alexandra, and Rachel. And for God's kindness in good times and bad, many thanks.

INTRODUCTION: A SHORT STORY ABOUT MY LIFE

This is a manual about freedom. *And* about being a nurse.

Some think that these two terms are contradictory. After all, being a nurse means being (take your pick) working in a facility you don't want to work in, working for people you don't want to work for, working *with* people you don't want to work with, working hours you don't want to work, doing things you don't want to do...you get the picture.

Since 1982, I have proved these all of these things wrong. And I am here to help you prove them wrong. To prove to you that nursing can be fulfilling, rewarding (financially and personally) and even—dare I say it?—fun.

You see, on December 27, 1982, I became officially self-employed in nursing. I was a free-lancer. I can remember that first day like it was yesterday. Because while it was something I'd wanted to do for a long time, there was that initial fear of doing something I knew of no one else doing. And the fear of making a fool out of myself. Or of failing, and going back to my old job at the hospital, and having to admit to everybody that my dreams were just that, dreams. Or of not making enough money to survive. (After all, I was a 25 year-old man in nursing, married, with a nine-month old son, and my family depended on me).

This was a dream I'd had since 1978, when I first began nursing school. Of being independent, self-employed, on my own. And when I finished nursing school in 1980, and went to work on a medical-surgical unit at a local hospital, I kept dreaming, and thinking about how I would do it, and whether I could indeed do it at all.

And finally in the fall of 1982, my wife and I left our son in the care of my parents and went to Pizza Hut, to sit down and map out a dream. And after an hour or two of eating too much pizza, we had realized that what with the small savings we had then, even if my worst case scenario came to pass, I could probably make it.

And I did. Not that there were not scary moments, times when it looked like it would all fly back up in my face. Not that there were not times when I would make stupid mistakes, and foolish decisions, and errors. But that's the wonderful thing about life. Sometimes even people who are stupid or don't really know what they are doing, turn out OK. And that was me. It could be you, too.

Let me assure you: I am no brighter than you, no more clinically skilled, lacking higher degrees, and not in a major metro area. For those who are wondering, I live about six miles from the house where I grew up, in a town of about 40,000 people. Now, I don't have *one* child, I have four. And I was not blessed with colossal amounts of money from family, or *any* of the things people sometimes suspect. What I am blessed with is the ability to dream. I knew what I wanted to do. I did not hate my job, and I did not despise my co-workers. The reasons I wanted independence were not negative, they were *positive*: I wanted freedom. Freedom to dream. Freedom to try. Freedom to fail (and fail I have, and I will tell you about them: nothing is more irritating to me than books that purport to tell you that the road to freedom is a golden one, uninterrupted by detours). Freedom to spend time with my children. With my wife. With my friends. Freedom to learn new things. Freedom to travel.

All of these things are important to me. But dreaming is the most important. And by dreaming, I don't mean some vague, ethereal thing. I mean deciding what you want, and going for it. I haven't reached all of my goals. There are probably many I won't reach. But let me tell you a philosophy I go by. I aim for the stars. I pick the biggest dreams I can find, and go for those. And perhaps I won't hit the stars. But wouldn't you guess that by aiming for the stars I just might hit a tad higher than someone who aims for the bathroom ceiling?

In a sense, that's what I'm hoping to give to you and all the other nurse readers of this book: a dream. I'm not giving you a blueprint. Your dreams, your plans, your backgrounds, your aspirations in nursing will all be different from mine. But if I can infuse you with a dream, you can chart your own course. And that's what I want to give you here.

Dreaming: How Visualizing Your Future Will Change Your Life

First, let me tell you a story. A woman had dreamed all her life of making a transatlantic ocean cruise. And she had done everything right for making that happen. She had saved for years, made all the right plans, determined the best ship to travel on. Everything was in place.

When the reservations were made, and the days slipped closer to when she would leave on her voyage, she began to pack. Nothing but the best would do for this trip! The best of clothes—the finest of everything.

One thing troubled her, though. She counted her money carefully, and realized that she had bought the best cruise she could afford, and while she was happy about that, it left little other money, for the extras for her trip. And one way she realized she could save was to scrimp just a little on food.

She knew! She would *pack* food for the trip. And so she did. All kinds of easy-to-prepare foods that she could quietly, easily, *frugally* eat in her cabin. When she went on the ship, there was a large package filled with canned tuna and olives and breads and crackers—and here, too, nothing but the best.

And it was a *wonderful* trip. She enjoyed the music and the shows and the fresh ocean breezes…oh, it was a wonderful trip. Her only regret was that she had to take leave of her new companions at meal times, going to her cabin to eat alone. They would always invite her to eat with them. But she knew—as much as she would like to—that there was no way for her to afford the meals in the dining room on her rather tight budget.

But the last night on ship was a festive one, and they would soon be in port. And the breezes were warm and dry, and she had spent the day having fun with her friends, and she thought through how much money she had, and she realized that there was enough—just enough, but enough—to splurge this one last night there on the ship, and so she accepted the invitation of her companions to dine with them.

And that night was perhaps the best of all. She enjoyed the finest of foods, and the happy conversation, and dancing, and realized that this had truly been a trip of a lifetime. And as she sat listening to the pleasant conversation, she knew it had been worth it. And when this best of evenings of this best of trips was over, she beckoned to the waiter, and quietly asked him for her bill for this wonderful dinner.

He looked puzzled. "Why, madam," he replied, "This meal is like all of your meals. The price was included in the cost of your ticket."

I am not a metaphysical person. I do not encourage people to dreams things that are truly beyond them. That can be cruel, like the speakers who act as though a crippled person could one day play in the Super Bowl.

But most of us live our lives like this woman, who walked to her cabin that evening, happy for a wonderful trip, but slightly sad that she had avoided so much that was there for the picking. We go through life, living in the most crimped, mean way that we can, thinking that life is some type of ration line, where we are being doled out the most meager of fare.

Sometimes life really does give us what we want. And that's what I want to talk to you about in this section…about finding out what you want. And what you are really about.

I wrote earlier about shooting for the stars. I mean that. Shooting for the stars is the way to get what we want. Most of us give up too soon. We settle for the most meager of life's offerings when the slightest obstacle occurs, not knowing that those obstacles are just part of the negotiating process.

Have you ever watched a good bargainer? The other party in the bargaining will throw up an objection, and the expert bargainer will listen carefully, and then deal with it. The bargainer doesn't think that an objection is the *end* of the process…she realizes it's just the *beginning* of the process.

But we treat life so differently. The slightest obstacle comes up, and we cave in, thinking that that is the end of the process, not knowing that life in a sense is a little game, almost a dance, and it's our turn to do our part of the dance.

I remember well the best negotiator I ever saw. It was 1995, and my son and I were in China, and we were visiting the Great Wall of China. And while China is still *officially* Communist, no one would ever know that from watching the behavior of the vendors on the mountainside down from the Great Wall. They tried to get us to buy something—*anything*—on the way up, and we begged off, not wanting to carry anything up the hill and down. But one persistent merchant spoke some of the few English words she knew: "I remember you!" (In other words, *"I will remember you!"*) And we went up the mountainside, and enjoyed seeing the Wall, and when we came back by her stall, she was as good as her word. "I remember you!" she shouted.

Well, suffice it to say that I hadn't planned to buy anything that day, but I did. I bought some cute souvenir T-shirts, one each for my three daughters, and one each for some nephews. But what was so amazing about the whole process was that I so enjoyed the banter that she was able to keep the whole purchase going with. And that's what a good bargainer does.

Sometimes a good dancer will react, or dip, or twist around, or any number of things, as part of the show, the fun, the wonder of it all. And we forget that life is a dance, that getting to our final destination can be a part of the fun of the destination.

The visit I made to the Great Wall was part of a trip my son and I took to Mongolia, that faraway country in northeast Asia, nestled between China and Russia. I had dreamed about this trip for years. To make a very long story short, I had been interested in Mongolia since I was 17. At that time, Mongolia was one of those die-hard Communist countries where travel was next to impossible. But the Communist government fell during that great wave of freedom that swept the world from 1989 to 1991, and I was free to go to Mongolia. And I began making plans. And there were lots that had to be made, because Mongolia is *still* difficult to get into, and travel there can be primitive.

The plans were not all that was involved. Getting to a place halfway around the world takes several days, even in a time of advanced air travel. So my son and I left Greensboro and flew to New York, and thence to Helsinki, and thence to Beijing, and from there to Ulaanbaatar, the capital of Mongolia.

And Mongolia was where I spent the next 2 weeks, and I had a ball. And Mongolia was obviously the goal and destination of this vacation.

But wouldn't it have been a shame if Mongolia was the only thing on my mind? Given that we were going through several of the world's major cities on the way, I made plans to enjoy them.

So in New York, we spent the afternoon with my sister-in-law. And in Helsinki, we toured the downtown area, and saw the harbor. And since we were in Beijing several days, we saw Tian an men Square, and the Great Wall, and all the other tourist hot spots.

The point that I am trying to make is that there are goals you have in your life—usually a couple of big ones. And you hope to get to those goals before your life is over. But the day-to-day stuff of life can be somewhat peripheral to those goals, but I hope that peripheral as it can be, you are still enjoying what you do along the way to those goals.

Life is a great big adventure. There will be twists and turns in the road we travel. Enjoy the changes and minutiae of life. But *never* take your eyes off the big goals. The big dreams that make you who you are. When obstacles occur or things we didn't quite expect to happen come along, accept those as part of the game or the dance of life. And enjoy them for what they are. But keep plugging. Try to discover how they can fit into your bigger goals. But don't let them keep you away from the dreams you have.

WHAT ARE YOUR DREAMS? (YOUR FIRST LIFETIME QUESTION)

If you are a reasonable person, by now you're thinking, "It's OK to talk **about** dreams, but what dreams is he talking about?" Fair enough. That's what this section is for. I want to show you how to set down your dreams and goals on paper, to refine them, and to make them truly yours. Putting them on paper is important. Goals not written down tend to ethereal, and not easily attained. Putting them on paper makes them concrete, at least for our minds. Putting them on paper gives us something to look at, something to aim toward, something to make our own. I have been writing down goals since I was a child. There are always some who look askance at writing goals, especially in one so young, and the one who wrote them always feels a bit foolish looking back on them, because so many of them are far-fetched, and unbelievable. But some of them I have accomplished. Some are still being worked on. But all of them gave me a place to go, a destination. If you and I begin trips at the same time, and I have a destination, and you have none, it is entirely possible I will not get there. My car may break down, I may get lost, a tornado may hit. But I can guarantee that you—without a destination, without a goal—will not make it. Because you have nowhere to go. And that's why I encourage goals.

Another reason for written goals is that it forces us to deal with the goals that sometimes seem far-fetched. Writing them down forces us to deal with the craziness of some of the things we want, and face them eye-to-eye.

And you wonder, why write them down at all, if the dreams are crazy, stupid, impossible to attain? Because they just may not be so crazy after all. And if it's impossible to get to that particular dream, perhaps there's a similar dream that you *can* do.

So before you read any further, get a piece of paper. Here's the first homework assignment (not the last, I guarantee) of this book. And please *do it*. Reading about dreams is not the same as writing them down, and writing them down isn't the same as *doing* them, but it's a good place to start.

Take a pen, a couple of pieces of paper, and put a title across the top: *Lifetime Goals*. Now give yourself two minutes, and start writing. Write down every crazy thing you've ever wanted to do. This is not the time to censor what you are writing. If possible, write without thinking about what you are writing.

Two things to remember. First, this is not a time to *only* list career goals. Certainly it's a *part* of what you should write, but not the only thing you should write. The reason I say this is because where you and your career go in nursing is not isolated from the rest of your life, and if—for example—spending more time with your children or grandchildren is one of your goals, that will have to dovetail with career goals. But, again, don't censor. Don't assume that two goals are contradictory, even though they may appear to be so at first glance. There will always be time to pare down your goals, to bring them into line with reality. This is not the time to do that. This is the time to let the birds fly in the air. Later on, you can put them back in the cage.

The other thing to remember is that your list should be *goals*, not *activities*. Most people confuse the two. *Earning a master's degree* is a goal; *going back to school* is an activity, or a means to the goal. Tell yourself what your destination is, *not* the means to get there. We'll work on the path to your goal later. It's like being in New York, and saying I want to get to Los Angeles. There are many ways to get there. I can fly, or drive, take a train, or walk. If I fly, I can take any number of airlines, different routes, different fares…you get the idea. What I want you to do is list the city you want to go to, so to speak. Although you will want to keep your goals general and abstract, remember to take into account all of the areas of your life: think about personal, family, social, career, financial, community and spiritual goals. And remember that your goals will be different, depending on the time of life when you're writing. A 12 year-old would have different life-time goals than would someone who was sixty. But with those reminders in mind, get started, go for it, and start writing.

EVALUATING YOUR DREAMS: WHERE WILL THEY TAKE YOU?

Now I assume you have just spent the last two minutes writing out all the crazy and not-so-crazy dreams that you have been harboring in your mind. (If you have *not* already done it, please do so now: the next section won't be much help otherwise).

Now that you've written your goals, give yourself an additional two minutes to refine and ponder your goals. You may also want to think about your life, and see if there are patterns of behavior that indicate a goal, even when you haven't thought about it explicitly. An example of this would be someone who has continued taking classes and earning degrees after finishing nursing school. Such a person probably has a goal of self-improvement. If you notice something of this nature, be sure and write that down, too.

Look honestly at your dreams. There may be many; there may be few. I hope you have been honest, and I hope you have not censored your dreams. Leave that for everybody else in your life. There will always be those around who can tell you that what you want to do is impossible, or that you are "only dreaming." But tell yourself on paper what you honest want, and what you are honestly hoping to achieve. It may be wild, it may be unusual, or it may be something you think you'll never be able to do. Perhaps so. But that's what dreams are for...giving you the chance to do more than you are right now.

The Second Lifetime Question

Now you have listed a number of goals. For most people, these goals are fairly vague at this point, including such things as "happiness," "children," "success," and "satisfaction." Now we're going to narrow it down a bit. Using the same parameters as we did before, I want you to take two minutes, and ask yourself: *How do I want to spend the next five years?* Again, write as quickly as you can and write as much as you can. Then take another two minutes to refine the answers you've given, and look for any patterns in your life right now.

The Third Lifetime Question

Now, we've thought about what you want to do with your life, and where you want to go. Now I would like to bring it in sharp focus. Give yourself two minutes, and ask yourself: *What would I do with my life if I had only six months to live?* (And by the way, this is a question about *living*, not about preparing to die. Assume that you've done all the necessary things: preparing a will, planning your funeral, etc.) Write quickly, but *write*. Don't get bogged down in the mechanics. Just write.

EVALUATION: PUTTING YOUR DREAMS INTO REALITY

Now give yourself a few minutes, and look at your answers. This is the beginning of what will probably be a lifetime process of evaluating where you are, and where you want to go. Ask yourself some questions: Do the answers I give in the first, second, and third sessions flow into each other? Or do I list goals in the first that are radically different from the second and the third? Am I honest with myself about what I really want? If my "six months to live" goals are radically different from the previous two lists, why am I not *now* living like that?

By the way, I'm not saying that you have to *do* all that you would like to do. I am not one of these writers who thinks you should, for example, abandon your children in search of personal fulfillment. What I *do* suggest is that you be cognizant of what you would like to do, brutally honest, even at the risk of saying, perhaps, that there are certain goals you will not be able to fulfill. I give two examples. One is a friend who desperately wanted to get into med school, but was unable—due to grades, mostly—to do so. I counseled him to think about what it was about being a physician that he wanted. I asked him if it was contact with the sick, or was it autonomy, or was it the adventure of curing illness. Any of these desires could be realized *in different ways* than the way he initial thought. For example, working with the sick could be achieved by a career in nursing, or by any number of jobs within hospitals or clinics. Autonomy could be achieved by a whole spectrum of self-employment opportunities.

15

The other example is my own. For several years, I had wanted to homeschool my children. However, my wife teaches at a community college, and I have my own practice, and I could not figure out a way to teach them without our giving up one or the other. Here is a time when I was too close to the patient to make a correct diagnosis. A friend suggested this compromise, which we implemented. I teach the children two to three mornings a week, and my wife (who teaches on a part-time basis) teaches them the other days. The system we worked out required some compromises and tradeoffs, but gave us the freedom to do our work, and be with our children as we wanted.

Both of these examples may be irrelevant to you, or they may be completely relevant. What I am saying is that your family and friends may be *parts* of your dreams, rather than hindrances to them.

(An editorial addition here: your children—if you are fortunate enough to have them, or if you are fortunate enough to have them come into your life in the future—are important. Consider them as gifts to *your* life, given for a short time, and then they move on, hopefully to remain in your heart, if not in your home. Enjoy them. Treasure their company. They have much to teach you, and no amount of success outside of the family will compensate for failure there. I am not talking about the relatively minor failures that we all go through every day. We are always failing those around us, and for that the only known cure is a steady stream of forgiveness, from you to them, and from them to you. But I *am* talking about the major failures. I am talking about a man I heard of who was playing golf with a younger friend. The man mentioned that his daughter had just turned 21, and would be married in a few weeks. The man was a great success, according to most standards. Wealthy, important, and powerful, and yet he lamented to the younger man that he had never taken the time to get to know his daughter, and that that was something he could never get back. But even if that rings true to you, consider that even most major failures are not permanent. Consider a goal of getting to know your children, even if they are older, and even if they rebuff your first few attempts. They are worth it, and so are you).

After you've evaluated what you've written, take each of the three lists, and prioritize them. On each one, list the most important goal as A-1, the second most important A-2, and the third, A-3. Now take all nine of those goals, and get a fresh piece of paper, and write "My most important lifetime goals are ..." and list them, three of them, again, the first A-1, and so on. This is your preliminary lifetime goals list.

It is important to remember that this is not written in stone. What you are doing today is a snapshot of where you are right now, and it will invariably change, as your circumstances change. You will need to update and revise your lifetime goals periodically. Some people use their birthday as a time to update and evaluate. For some reason, I have found New Year's day good for that purpose, perhaps because everyone else is chirping about resolutions. I am not talking about resolutions. I am talking about what I am and what I am doing with what I am. I also find it sometimes useful to get apart by myself and ponder what is going on with my life, and what progress I am making. Writers are frequently seen as creatures who cannot fail, and who never doubt. Not so here. I believe that life is best lived by charging ahead, and going at something I want until there is plainly a stone wall in front of me. When there are stone walls (and that occurs rather more frequently than I would like) I try to take time to walk (because I enjoy walking) and think about what I can do. Should I keep plugging away at this, despite the stone wall? Should I look for a detour? Should I pull back? Life is a creative journey, and failure is neither final nor terminal. It is—if you live any kind of life at all—*inevitable*, and you may as well remember that, and not let it get you down. The bigger question is *What will I do with this failure?* How will I respond? Where will I go? Will I roll over and play dead...or will I get up, dust the dirt off my clothes, and go on to the next try?

We are accustomed to viewing success and failure as being two ends of a spectrum. They are not. Failure is not the opposite of success. The opposite of success is *giving up*. Failure is simply living on the edge of our competence.

May you be so blessed as to have that as a permanent address! I find that I deeply admire people who have failed many times. They are often the world's most interesting and successful people, and often the most generous and kind, as well. If we allow ourselves to be taught by our failures, we can learn incredible things, and grow immensely in ways that people who define success as avoiding failure never do.

I have never forgotten the first job I applied for when I finished nursing school. It was *not* a staff nurse position, but rather that of director of inservice education. The nursing director at this particular hospital was kind enough to interview me. How she kept a straight face is beyond me, because I was so incredibly underqualified for the job. Nevertheless, she talked with me, and though she turned me down for the position (looking back, I would think she would have been insane had she offered it to me) she did offer me a staff position on a med-surg unit, which I took.

I am blessed with a certain amount of ballsiness, and that is a good example. Sometimes it is embarrassing, and sometimes people who are gutsy fall on their faces. I sometimes laugh that if I have a day without failure, I view that as a *real* failure. Go for what you want. Aim for the stars. You will fail frequently. But you will do amazing things, and lead a fun and exciting life. It is said that there is a Chinese curse which goes *May you live in interesting times*. But I view it as a blessing, a benediction as we close this section. I hope that you live in interesting times. And I hope that your career in nursing—as well as the rest of your life—will be one driven by all of your wonderful dreams. Go for it.

Goals and dreams are important, but you cannot *do* them. That's an important thing to remember. It is easy to forget.

If I want security as a goal, I cannot *do* security. I can decide that saving money is an activity toward that goal of security, and start saving $25 a week. I *can* do that.

Are you ready for another exercise? This time, we are dealing with activities—activities which will help you reach those goals you've set for yourself. You need to:

1. list activities which will help you reach your goals and
*2. set priorities which will help you decide which activities will help you most **now** in reaching your goals.*

Take another five minutes. List your A-1 goal at the top of the page, and start writing activities. The most important part of this exercise is to keep writing. Don't try to filter or censor your ideas. Instead, keep writing activities that will help you reach your goal. Don't allow yourself to be bogged down by the thought that you may not be able to do a particular activity. This is the time to be a little crazy and free. Let yourself go. Maybe a particular activity is beyond what you can do, but maybe it can, and I can guarantee that it will never happen if you don't at least contemplate it as a possibility. Write now, and edit later. Most of us edit our plans and our lives much too soon. Let's look at an example. If travel is a goal, list everything you can think of that you can *do* in regard to traveling. Where would you like to go? Who would you like to travel with? When would you like to go?

Follow the same procedure with your goals A-2 and A-3. Give each of them the full five minutes, and as before, keep writing.

And now you have three pages full of activities. I assume you do. If you don't, go back and do it. This is different from the textbooks you used in school, which were mostly theoretical exercises (not that there's anything wrong with a theoretical exercise): this is not theoretical, folks, this is real life, about you and what you are doing with the rest of your life. But assuming you've got your allotted three pages, spend another three minutes on each revising your activities. Add, delete, combine, consolidate and even invent new activities.

Now the time has come to stop being creative and imaginative, and to start being very hard-nosed. Look *realistically* at each activity, and ask yourself:

"Am I willing to spend five minutes working on this activity in the next week?"

If not, strike it off. Now. Be ruthless. There is no point in thinking that this is something you *ought* to do. Perhaps you should. But if you are unwilling to spend even five minutes on it, there's no point in keeping it on your list. Things left on your list when you have no intention of doing anything about them have a way of distracting you from the things you *are* willing to do. Don't allow yourself that luxury. You can always go back to the list, and as I have said before, you should. The list is not written in stone. This is not to say that the goals of your life are not important—if they weren't, you wouldn't be working through this manual. However, plans for achieving those goals should be changed and adapted as necessary.

Every day gives you an opportunity to move closer to your lifetime goals. The important thing is to get started *now*. Dreaming about what you can do with your life can be a lot of fun, but it accomplishes nothing. Select an A-1 activity, and plan to do it today. To keep down any possible discouragement, make it one of the activities you can accomplish quickly and relatively easily. Life is growth. You didn't start off in life running the four minute mile—unless you were vastly different from most children. No, when you were a toddler, you began cautiously walking along furniture, and finally, you took a few steps, and then you walked, and you're finally where you are now, and walking is an almost unconscious activity. What I'm saying is this: don't try to start off running. Pick an activity equivalent to furniture cruising—or even crawling. When you get comfortable with that, move on to running. Don't neglect the harder activities—just start off easy, and build your way up.

EVALUATING YOUR EXPERIENCE

One of the beautiful things about being a nurse is that there are so many work possibilities. There are a huge range of places: hospitals, clinics, schools, factories, in-home, and public health, to name a few. There is a large range of things you can do, or jobs you can fill. (We've listed some of those later on in this manual). But you will only do a few of those in your lifetime, and probably no more than a couple at a time. So it is important to narrow your list of things you would like to do, and that you are good at, and aim for those particular possibilities.

To begin this part of our exercise, take a blank piece of paper, and start listing jobs and functions you've enjoyed doing in nursing. Take fifteen minutes to do this, and try to think back on every job you've had. (If you're getting ready to graduate from school, or have limited experience, think back on what experiences you have had, and especially on clinical experiences you've had in school). This is a time to be *specific*. Don't list *being a staff nurse on unit 400*. Instead, list what *specifically* you liked about being a nurse on unit 400, or more specifically, what you liked *doing*. "Doing" would include something like, "I enjoyed wound care," or "I enjoyed interviewing new hires for our unit" or "I enjoyed teaching breast self-examinations." Like our lists in the other exercises, simply list and don't edit. Make the list as trivial as you need it to be. If you like giving bed baths, say so. Don't be afraid that what you're saying won't be important. This exercise is for you—not for sharing with anyone else, unless you choose to share it.

After you've finished your fifteen minutes, take another five to go over the list. You might find yourself wanting to expand on something listed, or to edit, consolidate, or define.

Now turn the coin over, and take fifteen minutes, and write down those things you disliked. Again, remember that this is for you alone. Don't feel embarrassed at what you write down. If you loathed getting a blood pressure reading, write it down. As before, take five minutes after your initial fifteen to refine your list. If you listed that you disliked patient care, expand on that a little. Exactly what did you dislike about patient care? the more specific you can be (whether positively or negatively) the more helpful these lists will be to you.

The reason I'm being a little tough about not censoring is that nurses seem to have this vision of nurses, and where they *as individuals* don't fit that stereotype, they tend to be very hard on themselves. This is a breakdown of the myth. See if you don't recognize it somewhere in the back of your mind. Nurses are women who selflessly care about others. Nurses never complain, and for that matter, never feel like complaining. Nurses never get irritated by patients, even when the patient is the biggest headache within 300 miles. Nurses enjoy doing the dirty work around hospitals. And finally, nurses do not deserve to be paid well, and would never *think* of asking for pay commensurate with their skills. Recognize that somewhere? One of the things I want to do in life is to make nurses realize that there are lots of options available. Options that allow you to work doing what you enjoy, where you enjoy it, with people you enjoy, at times and hours you enjoy, and—last but not least—for the pay you deserve. So be honest. What you are doing here is important!

You might also want to take five minutes to list things in nursing you've never done, but have always thought sounded interesting. If you've spent the last ten years in geriatric nursing, but always thought critical care sounded like fun, put it down on your list. And as I said earlier, don't be afraid to dream. There's *nothing wrong* with trying something, and finding out you don't like it. I've found that people who were interesting, fun, or accomplish a lot tend to make a *lot* of mistakes, and tend to have walked down a number of blind alleys. Mistakes and failures are not fatal, as long as you get up, pick yourself up, and go on with your life.

Now take another five minutes and list those things in nursing that you do well—whether this is your own evaluation, or the evaluation of a colleague or supervisor. Two rules for this exercise: 1) Don't be shy. This is the time to blow your own horn. And 2) be specific. I keep coming back to that because it is important—as you will see in the closing exercise of this section.

Now you've taken time to make four lists. These four lists are fairly concrete, not requiring a lot of imagination or creativity. *Now* for the creative and imaginative part. I want you to take a fifth page, and this time, write across the top, "My ideal day." On this page, use fifteen minutes, and write, in as much detail as possible, what an ideal day would be like. This list is for imagination and creativity. Don't censor yourself! For this exercise, I want you to describe an ideal day in its entirety. This one should encompass all of your life—friends, family, sports, hobbies, work, in short, *everything* that makes up your life. Most of us are afraid to imagine such a life, but it is an amazing way of finding out what you want.

Now that you've completed this page, take another (there is an end to this, I promise!) and head this one, "My ideal work day." The only limit on this page is that you are describing your ideal *work* day. Will you be working alone or with others? In an institution? In a home? In industry? Will you be doing patient care? Supervising others? Teaching patients? Teaching other nurses? Will you be doing "detail" work? Or doing long-range planning? Will you be in the geographical area where you are now, or another? Where would you *like* to be? A large city? A rural area? Another state, city, or country? Will you be working in a fast-paced environment, or some place with a slower, steadier pace? If you see yourself in a hospital or other similar setting, in what department do you envision yourself working? What type of patient population will be there?

The amazing thing is that for most people, this is a relatively easy exercise *if they are honest with themselves*. Most of us have a pretty good idea of what we would like to do, and it doesn't take much to get that out on paper. Just don't forget that a nursing career can encompass a lot of things. If you've got some crazy idea that your friends have always made fun of, this is the place to put it down. (And if you've got some crazy idea that you've been too embarrassed to tell your friends, then by all means, *get it on paper!*) Your friends won't be looking at this paper, unless you want them to. As I said earlier, most of us are long on editing and short on imagination. Just write, and keep on writing for the whole fifteen minutes. Describe in as much detail as you can the day that would make you happiest doing the career you've chosen.

Don't let it bother you that what is an ideal day today would have been different five years ago, and will be different five years from now. You're starting with now, so don't let that bother you.

Now that you've spent your time, take another five minutes to go over each list. As before, you might want to revise, add, or expand on your list.

Now it's time to do the old e-word, and evaluate what you've written. Look carefully at the lists you've made. Examine them carefully, and examine your life as it is now. There are several questions you should ask yourself, preferably on paper:

1. In what ways is this idea day like a present day in your life?
2. In what ways is it different from a present day?
3. Am I willing to make the changes needed to change a present day to an ideal day?

This is an important question to ask. If you are presently working in a nursing home, with an associates degree in nursing, and your idea day pictures you teaching critical care nursing in a university setting, there's no reason you can't do it *if you're willing to pay the price*. Getting your dream fulfilled can—in this case—be fulfilled with several years of educational time, and several years of experience. Paying the price can be tough. I never said that it wasn't. But the alternative may be living a life you didn't really want to live. And remember that we tend to think that the price is more expensive than it really is. For some perverse reason, we magnify difficulties, and imagine walls that are not there. Decide what price you are willing to pay, and pay it. And realize that the pricetag may not be as bad as you originally thought.

Positioning Yourself for a Successful Career

There is an old saying, related to eggs and baskets. Don't put all of the eggs into one basket. The old saying is correct. *Don't* put all of your earning needs into one career basket.

It is common to pooh-hooh this saying now, among business books. The logic is that by putting all your eggs in one basket *and watching that basket carefully*, you will succeed. The problem is that most of us don't know enough about what we are doing. Even more crucial, most of us don't have enough working capital (that is, money that we can afford to lose) to take the overriding risk that putting all of your eggs in one basket involves. I advise nurses—and anyone going into business for themselves—to consider making a couple of income streams part of your life.

"Income stream" is probably a new concept to you, but most of you are familiar with it. If you are employed somewhere, you have one and only one income stream. I am not knocking that, necessarily. But life and the world change, and sometimes rapidly. Nurses have been somewhat immune to job loss and downsizing in the last half of the twentieth century, but there is no guarantee that that will not change. It is always sad to read the story of a large business closing, because there is the inevitable story about the man who has been working there for the last thirty years, has never worked anywhere else, has few "outside" skills, and doesn't know what to do. What I am recommending is that you pick several income streams (out of the list of possible practice areas) and seek to make some living off of them all. There are many possible variations of this practice, but it boils down to not boxing yourself into one corner, and making that one area or company or skill your one means of making a living.

On this note, I'm even speaking to those of you who are wanting to remain in, say, a hospital setting. Going to a free-lance basis can have an upside you can't even imagine now. When a hospital—or any other employer—has an idea that they have you by the collar, and that you are severely unlikely to go anywhere, short of physical abuse, it is astonishing what they will put you through.

There is a great example here. When I had been in my own practice for a couple of years, I got a call from the director of nursing at a local extended care facility. She was asking me to free-lance on their medical unit, and I went to interview her, and she me. (A note about interviews: when you are independent, you must realize that setting up a mutually beneficial working relationship involves your interviewing, as well as being interviewed. You are not going there, hat—or cap—in hand, hoping that they will grace you with a job. You are going in as an equal, who will be providing services on a mutually agreeable basis. *Never forget this*). She explained the hours that she was seeking my services, and I tentatively agreed, and she asked what I would charge. I named my fee, and she gulped, but readily agreed. I knew that my fee was twice what the nurses I would be working with were being paid. I also knew the history of this institution. I had—several years before—had to examine the administrator of the facility. A particularly oily and disgusting man, he had boasted that it was his basic plan to pay nurses as little as possible, because that would ensure that they would be loyal. (Perhaps you can understand this logic, because I can't). The outcome of this policy, of course, ensured only that nurses would work there for the shortest time possible before going to another facility, or that the only nurses they were able to keep for any length of time would be the dregs of the profession, *unable* to find work elsewhere. Their needing to hire me—and being willing to pay me my usual fee—was the logical outcome of such a policy. The nursing director's plea was only that I not tell the other nurses what I was being paid, and I was agreeable to that. But for some reason, there were always nurses who would agree to work under such a policy (which he did not keep a secret). I find it professionally repugnant that nurses will agree to such arrangements, barring the most severe need on their part. Unless your next meal depends on getting a job *that day*, I suggest you get up and walk out if a policy like this comes up in an interview situation. You owe it to yourself and to the nursing profession to do so.

There are several downsides to this. The first is that you are unlikely to become rich (although I suspect you will make a very good income, probably considerably better than you are making now as an employee, not to mention that you will have freedom that you do not now have). Getting rich, or the possibility thereof, comes later, when you've developed self-employment skills and some capital in the form of savings. At that time, you will know what you are good at, and you will know that niche where you can specialize. But for now—when you are just beginning—pick several areas—I suggest five—and go with all of them. The second downside to going with five areas is that you are less likely to become an expert when dividing your time among several areas. A crack critical care nurse becomes that way by study and intense devotion to a specialty area. But again, that kind of specialization can come later, when you have discovered your strengths and have the ability to sort out where you can best go. But for now, go with the very good choice of being a free-lance generalist, and realize that nursing can be a whole new form of adventure. Take what you have learned about yourself as a person, and what you have learned about yourself as a nurse from our exercises above, and choose five income streams to make your work life.

I did that when I started out in 1982. I was going to do all of these, and I did: free-lance paramedical exams, private-duty nursing, free-lance staffing, free-lance agency home health, and private home health. (This gives you an idea of what you can learn when you're out on your own: I was under the illusion that home health care nursing was something one could do on one's own. In a few months, I realized that this is a big under-taking, requiring other staff, offices, billing departments, and 24 hour care. But I tried). Unless you are blessed with a great deal of knowledge about business and know exactly what will work for you, and what won't—and most of us aren't very knowledgeable about business—I sug-gest you pick five areas, and go with them. On at least one, you will know that you have completely overshot the mark, and you will realize that it is totally beyond what you can do. But two or three—probably four—will work. And they will allow you to enjoy your life, give you more freedom, grow as a nurse, and be your own boss. Allow yourself the freedom to fail. Those who are afraid to ever fail usually end up being the employees of someone who *isn't* afraid to fail.

Getting Business to Come to You

At the risk of over-simplifying, the way to get business is to ask for business. While most people admit to being terrified of public speaking, the fear induced by the simple word "sales" surely is a close runner-up. And yet that is what I am asking you to do. That's what sales is: asking for business. Asking people to buy your service, to rent your time, to use your expertise. Sale is *not* inducing customers or clients to buy something they don't want or need, and it is not begging people to buy. At its simplest, it is showing a potential customer or customers what you have to offer, and inviting them to buy. And often it is as simple as that. It can be enormously complex, but it can be astonishingly easy. It is not the place for modesty or downplaying what you have to offer. I am amazed by what most nurses know. They are highly skilled professionals, but how many of us wouldn't be a lot richer than we currently are if we had a dime for every time we've heard a plaintive "I'm just a nurse …." These words are spoken every day by men and women who save lives, bring happiness, alleviate pain, and put lives back together. Just a nurse? Banish that phrase from your vocabulary!

I cannot give you a definitive word on how you will get business, because there are so many ways which you can *do* a nursing career. A couple of suggestions for you, though. The first is that if you have a business card, you are 90% in business. If you don't believe me, just think about how much more respect you show someone's business idea if she has a simple card with her name and phone number. There's no reason you should be any different. *You need to have a business card.* It can be simple or it can be fancy, but you need one. If your funds are limited, get the most inexpensive card available, but get one. They are now incredibly cheap—at a place like Office Depot, you can usually get 1,000 cards for $10 or $11. And when they are this cheap, you can afford to throw them around. When I opened my practice, I went through a thousand cards a year, and I should have gone through more. I would always give people more than one—I'd usually give them five or ten. "Pass the extras on," I would say, "And if you don't know of anybody else, just throw the extras away." It was amazing. People would stick my cards in their files (they always do) and they would indeed pass them to others who needed my services. At a penny apiece, what do you care if they do throw them away? Do you think you can possibly risk the extra nickel it might cost you, on the chance that someone might pass the card to someone who might give you hundreds or thousands of dollars of business?

Places like Office Depot (and I'm not picking on them; there are dozens of such establishments, all good, and all cheap) are also good for brochures. And the wonderful thing is that they are not only printers, but they will also (usually at no extra cost) help you design the brochures. Don't be afraid to pick their brains, and use their expertise to your advantage. That's what they are there for, and they are usually happy to do it. Likewise, use their knowledge when designing stationery and envelopes.

The important thing is to be lavish in giving out your cards and brochures. They cost almost nothing, and they provide an amazing amount of leeway for getting into doors that might otherwise be closed to you. If you are still working at a hospital or clinic while you get your practice running, give cards to nurses and physicians you work with. 99% of them will admire your guts, and you will be amazed at how much people will go out of their way to help you, and pass your name on to others. Just don't be shy. You've got a good thing going. Make sure others know about it.

A Brief Word about Equipment: What You Need, and What You Don't

Unless you are different from me and 99% of the readers of this book, your funds are limited. You're sitting there, facing the prospect of leaving that comfortable old job where (despite any complaints you might have with it) you have a steady paycheck and starting off in a business or practice where you have no definite assurance of money from one day to the next. And *then*, there is the question of equipment. You *are* going to need equipment. It will, of course, vary depending on your specialty area, but you will need it.

The first tactic in reducing stress in a new situation is to put down a concrete list of what you're afraid of. After you've decided on an area of practice, you need to make a list of what you will need. When I began on my own, I didn't do this, and went to my first appointment taking my equipment in a paper bag. Yes, you heard that right. Fortunately, my wife pointed out that this was not a particularly confidence-inspiring image, and I changed it.

If I had thought about it, I would have realized that I needed a stethoscope, a sphygmomanometer, scales, a tape measure, a clipboard, and some urine dipsticks. To carry it all, I needed a briefcase. Now I am convinced that everyone, no matter how lowly their calling, should have a briefcase. For men, they serve as that convenient repository that women usually use a purse for. For women, they project a decidedly more professional image than a big, chunky purse, so get one, whoever you are. And put away any ideas you might have about buying one of those heavy, ugly, expensive semi-suitcases the lawyers carry around on TV soap operas. Instead, get a cloth, soft-side briefcase. They are great, and unlike the leather ones, expand if you need to put more inside. They also cost a lot less.

I bought all of that equipment new. what I got was of medium quality, not cheap junk, but at the same time not such high quality that I worried about losing it, or having it damaged. A reasonable rule of thumb might be that if something costs less than $50, it is not worth your time to search for it used. Don't go around trying to buy a used stethoscope when a serviceable one is available for $20 (and yes, that one will work find, at least for the practice I'm in. Another rule of thumb: don't buy a cardiology quality piece unless you need a cardiology quality piece...)

For more expensive equipment, plan to spend a little more time, and you may be able to get some nice equipment for a good price. Don't be ashamed to tell people that you are just starting out, and you want to buy something used for a good price. At the same time, find out what the retail prices are, so you will have a point of comparison. (Something to remember: Americans are very fond of small businesses. People are often eager and willing to help you. I am not suggesting that you be a mooch, only that you realize that you have a leg up on, say IBM. Whether it is in procuring equipment *or* advice, don't hesitate to use this to your advantage).

Try the following:

1. Calling physicians' offices, clinics and hospitals in your area. Explain to them that you are in the market for used equipment. Businesses are constantly getting rid of used equipment that is not necessarily damaged, just old. You may be able to get some very nice stuff for even nicer prices.
2. When you call these offices, ask them who repairs their equipment. Repair services often take in equipment, and may be able to sell you some.
3. Call area auction firms, and ask to be placed on their mailing lists. I bought my centrifuge at an auction held when a local

doctor retired, closing her practice. There was no one else interested in the centrifuge, and I got it for $2. I started the bidding at $2, but I guess I could have bought it for $1 or even 50 cents if I'd thought about it.

4. If you are doing contractual work for a company, they may have a group purchase plan, a leasing arrangement, or even better, they may provide equipment for you at no charge. I used to do some contracting for a company, and I needed an EKG machine. Because I bought it through them, I got it for $1,000, but that was $400 off the then retail price. I'm contracting with a different company now, and they provide a machine at no charge. Sometimes things just get better.

All of these are just ideas. Let your imagination loose, and you may be able to come up with others. The main point to keep in mind is that you want to get equipment that is functional and inexpensive. This is not the time to be prissy about looks. If I want beauty, I'll buy art for the wall, but when something does the job, and I'm the only one seeing it, I'll live with less than sterling looks. Any number of local firms would have been happy to sell me a new centrifuge, complete with a pretty shine, a 30 day warranty, and a manual. They would have also charged $200—300 for it. for $2, I can afford a little ugliness.

The same principles (buy function, buy inexpensive) can apply to equipment you have to buy on an ongoing basis. Make it known to your suppliers that you are always in the market for things that will costs you less and do the job just as well. Stay on the lookout for sales on such items as envelopes, tape, paper, computer ribbons, and other items that must continually be replenished.

EARNING YOUR LIVING OUT OF YOUR HOME

When I began working at home in 1982, I was just on the beginnings of a big crest of homeworkers throughout the 1980's and '90's. When I started out, it was seen as a mad novelty, the answer to all workplace problems, and the salvation for those disgruntled by workplace politics.

However, as millions of people began to work at home, it became less and less of a novelty, and became—as it should be—just another option for our working lives. It is decidedly *not* the answer to all workplace problems, nor is it the sure cure for those disenchanted with workplace politics. And—to burst the illusions of many who view it with envy in their neighbors—it is not for everyone.

It can be tough. If you are a social creature (I am not) you may find yourself missing the easy companionship of fellow nurses, even if you find yourself hating their very sight at times. If you need a group of people working together toward a common goal to get yourself motivated to work, you may find the sometime loneliness of working at home maddening. If you like the sounds and noises of a regular workplace environment, you may be frustrated by the utter silence that sometimes envelops you. And finally, if you just don't work well on your own, or find it difficult to get motivated without some direction (and there's nothing wrong with being that kind of person), you will likely hate working at home.

On the other hand, if you enjoy the texture of solitude, or get tired of the groupthink that sometimes pervades workplaces, or if you are self-motivated, and feel tied down by the slack work habits of some of your fellows, working at home may be for you.

As I said, I enjoy the challenge of working by myself, and working for myself. When I began, I was almost evangelical about the subject, an earnest spokesman for working at home. But people are very different, and that is one of the beauties of the human race. If you are one of those beings who thrive on a slightly different atmosphere, I encourage you to consider a home office.

There are millions of Americans and Canadians working out of their homes and apartments. You have probably dealt with a company by phone or mail order which you envisioned to be sitting in a large office complex, and in reality, the owner answered the phone while she was still in her pajamas. I know a woman who ran a successful nursing agency out of an office off of her living room. We are fortunate that technology has been so kind to those of us working at home. With computers, voicemail, fax technology, and numerous other advances, it is possible for the homeworker to operate on a much level playing field, and to compete successfully, sometimes with companies vastly larger than their own operation.

We are also blessed with differences in attitudes. When I began in 1982, home offices were viewed as something of an oddity, and sometimes with suspicion. Now, those working at home have become so commonplace that they are hardly noticed. I live on a court with four houses. I am the only homeworker on my court, but just around the corner lives a woman who publishes a successful local magazine out of her home.

You will also be astonished at the variety of nursing careers that can be home-operated. If you would like to work at home, consider several times before you rule out a particular career choice for a homeworking office. Most people I know would have laughed at the idea that a nursing agency could be run out of the home, but the woman I mentioned earlier pulled it off. And if you don't want to advertise that you are a one-person home office, advances in voicemail technology have made it amazingly easy to *seem* much bigger than you are. I am not suggesting deception, but if yours is a career that seems to demand a huge office complex, the technology will make your home office more palatable to your clients.

SPECIALTY AREAS FOR YOUR NURSING CAREER

There are, literally, hundreds of specialty and sub-specialty areas in nursing. You will, obviously, only pick a couple of these, but there are one or two or three that are really *right* for you, and you should take advantage of them. Of course, I won't be listing all of the possible specialty areas. Some I don't know (there: the first time you've ever seen an humble author) and others *I* think are not important. I emphasize the "I" because I am not the fount of wisdom of knowledge for nursing. I know what I have done, and I know what nurses have to bring to the marketplace, but I do not know everything. (In fact, I appreciate your input. If I've made a mistake, or if there's something you think I could have done better, write and tell me. My email address is *huffmanjim@hotmail.com.* If you think something is important, and I haven't mentioned it, write and tell me why. I will listen to you and hear your ideas. I am not the smartest guy around—far from it. It's just that I am willing to listen, to be corrected, and to learn, and I have found few things that are so good for your life as those three.

Also realize that nursing at the end of the twentieth century and the beginning of the twenty-first is—like the rest of life—changing a great deal. The way to keep on top of things in your professional career is by keeping your eyes and ears open to changes, and thinking about how you can react to those changes, and how you can better yourself by them. The other plus side is that things that improve *your* life will also improve the lives of your patients, and they will *improve the lives of other nurses.* Even though there were few nurses doing what I do when I started doing it, there were *some*, and I took great heart and encouragement from those brave pioneers. Most nurses who benefit will never tell you about what a difference you made in their lives, but take heart: what you are doing is important. And being brave, and bold, and daring is important, too. Often in ways you will never know.

Some specialty areas I'm not mentioning because they are only locally relevant, or because there are literally so few nurses who do them that I think there's little point in discussing them. But again, I see through a certain point of view, and I could be wrong. But regardless, the point of these lists is to give you ideas. You may come up with a sub-specialty that works well for you. Just read them, think about them, and let your imagination run a little freer than perhaps it has in the past.

The other area I'm not mentioning too much are those "obvious" specialty areas like anesthesia or various nurse-practitioner specialties. Not that I don't think these are important: not at all. The trailblazing work of many of these nurses throughout the years allowed nurses like myself the freedom to practice on our own terms. It's just that these are not what most nurses are aiming for. They also (most of the time) require extensive *formal* training, while I have concentrated on areas most nurses are at least legally *already* qualified to do, and many of which nurses can learn through internships, preceptorships, on-the-job training, or with some fairly quick and inexpensive continuing or other such education.

And for those nurses who are already in one of those specialty areas, a word of advice. If you are happy in your field, I'm glad for you. Keep working with this manual, because many of the suggestions I've given will be useful for you in your practice. However, if you slightly *un*happy, read on. I've seen more nurses than I care to remember who thought a particular specialty area would be enjoyable, but found out otherwise. (And lest you think otherwise, this is not confined to nurses: I can remember like yesterday going out to lunch with a bunch of lawyers. There must have been eight or nine of them, and I was the only nurse there. In fact, I was the only non-lawyer there. We went around the table and introduced ourselves, and I explained briefly what I did. One of them looked sad. "That sounds like fun," he said, "Wish I could do something that was fun.") If you are unhappy in your practice area, I would encourage you, like I would encourage this lawyer: consider making a change. Some will argue that they have already spent *lots* of time, energy, and money in learning a specialty. Perhaps you are still paying off debts on specialty training. But life is far too short. If you are really unhappy, chalk that time up to experience, and start looking for something else to do. Let's say you are thirty. You're probably going to be practicing for another thirty or thirty-five years. So what if you have "wasted" a year? Better to realize it now than to waste another thirty doing something you don't want to do. Besides, you have not wasted your time. What you learned in that training will be valuable no matter where you go, even if not directly. I'm not here to be your cheerleader, but life is not a punishment to be endured because you made a wrong call earlier about something you *thought* you would enjoy or be good at. One of the sure signs of winners is that they allow themselves the freedom to make mistakes, and then *they refuse to wallow in those mistakes*. Winners—long-term winners, that is—are almost always short-term losers many times over, much more so than the rest of us are. The secret is that they get up, and keep going. The other secret is that by making mistakes over and over and over again, they tend to learn what works and what does not. Many people are so afraid of making a mistake that they avoid them, and thus have no chance to learn from them. I am not saying that mistakes don't hurt. They do—tremendously. And the greater the mistake, the more pain involved. But they are an inevitable part of life, and the amazing thing that you will find is that most people who try really hard to avoid mistakes make about as many as those winners I spoke about. The problem is that most people make the mistakes, and keep beating themselves over the head for making them. What distinguishes winners is that they give themselves a time to hurt, and then they quit. Most of us—nurses are no exception—think that a mistake is a sentence that we are supposed to stay with forever. Ridiculous! Get up, shake the dust off, and keep going.

NURSING BUSINESS IDEAS REQUIRING NO MONEY (OR ALMOST NONE)

I am assuming that any nurse in the US or Canada can scrape together one or two hundred dollars, so I am not being completely truthful when I call it "no money needed." In any business idea, you will need to have a little money for such things as business cards, and some minimal equipment, a briefcase, etc., so plan on that. The most amazing thing about people who are really, truly broke—and most of us get into that position at some point or another in our lives—is that it makes us more resourceful and innovative, so if you are really scraping the bottom of the barrel, give yourself some time to think, and often you will come up with money resources that you did not know existed. I also encourage you to allow your present nursing position to fund your new venture. Even if you are working full-time at another nursing position, you can make time for your new career. Consider giving yourself—as an investment in your future—another eight hours (another work day, that is) of work a week, on your new career. Nursing can be especially kind on this, unlike some fields. If you need to work odd hours—say nights at a hospital—that will allow you some flexibility with your daytime hours. (I am *not* suggesting that you don't sleep. That is not a good idea!) If you think your time is all spoken for, ponder some areas where you might cut back. Are you willing to give up TV? Are there clubs or other activities that you are no longer enjoying that you could give up?

A word as to my definition of "nursing." At this stage in our professional development, there is no commonly accepted definition of what it means to be a nurse, or to do nursing. I am not sold on how valuable those definitions are to the working practitioner, anyway, so my ballpark definition of nursing is this (and which is in the back of my mind while I'm working on this manual): *nursing is any work situation in which the nurse is called a nurse, and considers what he or she does as nursing.* There are those who will sniff at this being a bad definition, and they are probably right. However, I think too many nurses (and this includes the theoreticians who are working on definitions of nursing) are too quick to box themselves in as to what nurses do. Allow yourself some freedom, allow yourself some working room, and allow yourself to be what you want without paying attention to some of the timeservers who think they are there to define what nurses should be.

All that having been said, here is our list of "no capital" nursing specialty/business ideas. Some will be ones you are familiar with, others not. It is not meant to be comprehensive, but rather to be a catalyst to give you some more ideas. Read it carefully, and use it as a launching pad for your own ideas and imagination.

AIDS/HIV nursing
Hospice nursing
discharge planning
utilization review
pain management
cancer nursing
organ transplant specialist
chemical dependency nursing
alcohol abuse nursing
diabetes nursing
eating disorder nursing
smoking termination clinics/seminars
occupational health nursing
ostomy care nursing
dietary consulting

medical/legal consulting
continuing education/inservice specialist
nurse recruiting
nurse recruiter consulting
birth coaching
labor and delivery nursing
insurance paramedical examinations
nursing resumes
pediatric nursing
neonatal nursing
adolescent nursing
critical care nursing
emergency nursing
geriatric nursing
infection control
orthopedic nursing
industrial consulting
school nursing
health product sales (to hospitals, other health facilities, the public,
or stores)
pharmaceutical sales
drug screening
hospital computer coaching
industrial alcohol and drug consulting
home health care
private duty care (surgical, long-term patients, hospitals, SNF's, ICF's,
and hospice)
image consultant for nurses
nursing consultant for architectural firms
neurological nursing
pulmonary nursing
free-lance agency nursing

sports screening
sports medicine nursing
"elder checks"
consultant on elderly care
consultant on child care
nurse career consultant
music therapy
medical-surgical nursing
in-home child care
Travel nursing: hospital staff relief
Air travel nursing
writing books and for nursing publications
hospice nursing
care of the handicapped
oncology nursing
opthamalogy nursing
boat travel nursing
multi-level sales of health products
medical office nursing
public health nursing
nurse consultant to television and films
on-site nursing (for example, on construction sites)
camp nursing

Is this giving you some ideas? I hope so. But keep reading. I'm going to talk briefly about these ideas, and I hope again that this will whet your imagination and creativity to help you get your nursing career going where you want it to go.

Let me also encourage you to know that there are willing collaborators in your plans, and you should make use of them. It took me years to realize that there are many individuals and companies that needed my services, and I could benefit from them as well. I am talking about such companies as nursing agencies, home health agencies, paramedical examination companies, and medical equipment suppliers. As you know, I encourage nurses to provide themselves with *multiple streams of income.* If you are working for a doctor's office, and that is your only source of income, and something happens and that office closes, you are—at least temporarily—sunk. In effect, you had *one* stream of income, and someone dammed the stream! Becoming dependent on one stream of income also makes you more fearful, and more inclined to put up with obnoxious, bossy, and demanding employers, because they rightly perceive that you have *nowhere else to go.* It is astonishing how much more respectful and—to use as a current buzzword—collegial—people become when they know that they cannot treat you badly, or you will quickly take your business elsewhere. You must realize something about your career: if you put up with someone who treats you disrespectfully, if you allow someone to put you down, if you permit someone to minimize your nursing judgments, *it is no one's fault but your own.* The sad thing about such a situation is that nurses who put up with this kind of thing make the situation bad, not only for themselves, but for other nurses as well. Don't be guilty of doing this.

It's also important to realize that you are a customer of those you do work for. If I went into Wal-Mart, and was treated rudely and disrespectfully, I would probably take my business elsewhere. I am not advocating being hyper-sensitive, and jumping ship when someone has a bad day, but I encourage any nurses who are being badly treated to quickly take their business elsewhere...go do your work for someone else!

Of course, this works both ways. Those you work for are *your* customers as well. If you treat them badly, fail to show common courtesy, or are rude, they have the right to take their business elsewhere, too. I have a vision of nurses who are sharp professionally as well as being warm, caring, and courteous men and women. Both can be true.

But I mentioned those willing collaborators, and here they are. If you are interested in free-lancing in hospital or nursing home type facilities, there are almost certainly nursing agencies in your area which would be interested in your services. I suggest you call all of them, and mention that you are planning to free-lance, and would be interested in possibly coming on board with them. *Make sure you mention that you are calling a number of agencies.* The reason for this is what I mentioned above. Human nature being what it is, the people in these agencies will treat you better if they know that you have the option to go elsewhere with your business with a minimum of hassle. That having been said, let me assure you that most of these people are good to deal with. I have dealt with a number of agencies over the years, and the troublemakers have been few. Most of the people are good and professional, and will go out of their way to make things work with you. Most of these sort of agencies also do private duty care cases, and you might want to suggest that you are available to do those, too.

If you have interest in almost any type of home care, you should also call the home health agencies, most of which will be listed in your telephone yellow-pages under "Home Health Agencies" or "Nurses." These agencies provide intermittent care (meaning, the nurse does not stay continually with the patient, but goes, provides the needed care, and leaves) to home-bound patients. There are many varieties and types of these agencies, and while some of them operate by employee nurses, many of them have opportunities available for contract nurses (meaning, you get paid for each individual visit which you make). In contract situations, you set your own hours, and can often earn more money than if you were employed, while at the same time working *less* hours.

Another useful collaborator is the paramedical examination facility. These companies provide paramedical examinations by nurses (usually done in the home or office of the person being examined) for insurance companies. The persons who are examined have applied for life, health, disability, or long-term care insurance, and various examination services are needed. Some will need a paramedical exam (health history, blood pressure and pulse rate, height and weight), some a blood and urine specimen, some an EKG, and many some combination of these requirements. These facilities are almost always in need of nurses, and I encourage you to contact several of them, and find out about what they need, and what they can offer you.

Please let it be understood that I am *not **necessarily** suggesting* that you should contemplate a long-term career with any of these type of companies. It's just that they are used to working with free-lance nurses, and may allow you to get your feet wet in "non-employee" nursing. That is no small thing. There are some people who begin—to use an example—their mountain climbing by hiking up Everest. While Mt. Everest may be a worthy goal, it is not the place to begin. Instead, we should respect our nature as human beings, and realize that a small and tentative step is a good place to start: something like the way a baby begins walking. Begin with the small steps, and you are allowing yourself to learn from your—*inevitable*—mistakes, when those mistakes will not hurt nearly so bad. This is a good thing.

On the other hand, one of these organizations might be just your cup of tea, and if you enjoy this type of nursing, and it gives you the freedom and money you need, go for it. There are usually no rules in this career game, except those you impose on yourself. You are in for a big adventure. Buckle up for the ride!

Here is a summary of some of the areas where you can practice nursing. It is not exhaustive. It *is* designed to give you room to think. Most of us focus our lives far too narrowly, when the secret of an interesting life consists in thinking outside the box, and looking for opportunity where most people see no opportunity. Or they notice only problems, and most problems are merely opportunities in disguise. Give yourself time to think, ponder, and enjoy the wonder of this world.

HOSPITAL NURSING AND OTHER AREAS

Hospital nursing is the area most of us are familiar with from the beginning, and it's the one where most nurses think of their careers, at least in the beginning. I start here because it is familiar, but also because the hospital is such a far-ranging place of opportunity, and most nurses are unable to see it. In a large city hospital, virtually every nursing specialty will be represented, and new specialties are coming on board every day. In 1980, for example, few had heard of what we came to term AIDS, and no one had conceived a nursing specialty dealing with the syndrome, but there are many nurses who make it their life's work every day. In addition to the multitude of clinical specialties, there are many other non-clinical (that is, not hands on) specialty areas represented. In few other facilities will there be specialists devoted to such areas as discharge planning or utilization review. There is the chance to work in a team (for example, on a medical-surgical unit), on a modified team approach (in critical care units), as a solo practitioner (in primary nursing units), or as a consultant to other nurses about *their* patients (in such areas as pain management or ostomy care). There is also the opportunity to consult with other nurses about themselves in some facilities as a occupational health nurse, employee assistance, and inservice education. This is not to mention the various layers of management positions open for those who have the gift, skill, and love for making a facility hum like a top. If you are an adventurer, there are areas like flight or helicopter nursing, and if you enjoy being more of a generalist, smaller hospitals give you the ability to keep up with a number of areas—often in the same workday! Hospital nurses are also given the unique ability to learn wide-ranging skills when they are newly graduated from nursing school, or coming back from a career hiatus. In short, hospitals provide a fertile ground for nurses to exercise their skills while at the same time becoming independent, free, and doing what they want to do.

ICF/Extended Care/ Long-Term Care Facilities/Nursing Home

These type of facilities go under a number of names. They can range from places that give care that would have been comparable to an acute care hospital just twenty years ago (owing to changes in Medicare and other insurance rules, patients are—as you are no doubt aware—being discharged from hospitals *much* sooner than previously was the case) to very informal care centers—where almost all of the care is being provided by minimally-trained staff—for mildly ill elderly or handicapped residents having no other place to live and no one else to care for them.

Many of the same opportunities are available here as in hospitals. Some of these facilities are large, complex structures, and have enormous needs for nurses. Nurses who specialize in care of the elderly or handicapped are especially needed for the long-term care aspects of patients in these facilities. There is usually a special need for good managers in such facilities. You will often find that you will be giving relatively minimal hands-on care, but will instead be directing a team of staff—sometimes other nurses, but usually nurses' aides/assistants, orderlies, or patient care technicians—who will be doing the hands-on care. Of course, there are treatments that only you as a nurse can give, and you will be responsible for those. But management is a great and needed gift, to encourage a sometimes disheartened and burned-out staff who work hard, often with minimal pay, benefits, and recognition. Many of the staff members you will be working with will have been there for many years, and they provide excellent care, especially when the managing nurses recognize that, and recognize *them*. A word of advice: in such a situation, be a little generous with praise.

Home Care

While home care has always been a component of nursing, in recent years it has come into its own as a special practice area. Proponents of home care have always argued that it was cheaper to care for many people in their own homes than to force them to be institutionalized—not to mention the benefits to your patients. In-home care is often done on a per-case basis, in which the nurse will be making visits to a number of homes throughout the day. Another component of home care is the care by private-duty nurses on a long or short-term basis. Nurses will also find career opportunities in such fields as in-home child care (it's surprising how reassured parents can be when their children are cared for a nurse) or in-home elderly care. Specialists in health teaching will find the home to be a fertile area for their practice, since much of the teaching done while the patient is hospitalized must be adapted to the patient's home situation. There are also many non-residential hospices providing care for dying patients on an at-home basis. We can safely say that home care has just begun to grow. In the years to come, home care will be growing. Nurses who enjoy freedom and flexibility on an informal basis will often enjoy this area of care.

Public Nursing

OK, so "public nursing" is not a very good title. I agree with you. But what I am talking about under this heading are services offered by you as a nurse to the public, without them having to go through the intermediary of an institution or another provider. This is one of those areas where this is a huge *potential* demand, but few nurses are offering such services. For many years, I made my living—and a quite good one, I might add—by such a service: I was a nurse paramedical examiner, providing examination services for insurance companies. But the possibilities in this field are so large, and the potential so vast, you should allow yourself a bit of time to consider them all. The demand in the specialty I picked has grown tremendously in the last decade, and yet insurance companies often have trouble finding nurses willing to do something that is enjoyable and pays quite well. Nurses need to realize that they are both needed and respected, and they should take advantage of that situation. In such areas as childproofing homes (ensuring that a house is safe for a newly arrived, or soon-to-be arrived baby), elderproofing (likewise for a newly handicapped or disabled elderly or not-so-elderly person), nurses can provide both the expertise along with the comfortable feeling that the nurse is really looking out for the client's needs. There's also demand for such things as in-home or at-the-office blood pressure checks, and other such services. The sky is quite literally the limit in this broad area where nursing can be performed. We are letting ourselves down as individual nurses as well as a professional group when we don't think about what we can do to provide services here.

Office Nursing

If you enjoy a slower pace of nursing practice, or simply need a respite from the insanity that sometimes pervades hospital practice, consider working within the confines of a medical or other office. I am not only talking about being "Dr. Jones' nurse" (although that is certainly a valid area of work). I am talking about practicing whatever specialty you enjoy in a medical practice.

This may require some innovation. It is possible that whatever practice you would like to work for has never considered having, for example, an ostomy nurse on board. And yet your specialty area may be enormously beneficial to the patients of that practice, and you in turn may benefit the other health professionals working there by providing your skilled expertise and teaching ability on staff.

The larger the office, the easier the sell. If you are talking to an office where there is one physician, a receptionist, and a janitor, the doctor may find it hard to believe that your presence would bring in enough revenue to justify your salary. On the other hand, a multi-specialty complex with two hundred physicians may have an office manager who sees the benefits right away.

There are no hard and fast rules here. Some large offices are gargantuan, complex, and unable to innovate in the slightest, while some smaller practices will be able to move quickly and see your arguments without difficulty. Have your points spelled out in advance, at least in your mind, and be able to prove why your presence on staff would benefit their profitability. (Assuming they are for-profit, and not a charitable organization. Bring some of the same arguments to a charitable organization, only this time you should stress how much your skills will be of service to their patients or clients). The skills and talents of nurses are not superfluous, but are rather highly beneficial to the needs and wants of your patients. Be ready to prove your point.

Services to Other Nurses

Nurses think that the only way they can do nursing is when they are providing services to the general public, and the only way nursing can be "done" to other nurses is if the nurse in question is having an appendectomy done! Not true! A vastly overlooked area is providing services to other nurses. Although there's nothing wrong with it, I'm *not* talking here about clinical services, but rather about services that enhance the lives and careers of your professional colleagues.

Most of these opportunities are in the education and consulting areas. Some nurses are serving a niche market for hospital education and inservice education for small hospitals and extended care facilities which have difficulties keeping a full-time educator on staff. These nurses provide the same services on a free-lance basis, at a much cheaper cost to the institutions, and thereby allowing their colleagues at these facilities to keep current on professional developments. Other nurses provide free-lance nurse recruiting, or they consult with other nurse-recruiters about improving *their* services. If you're handy with writing, there is a great need for nurses who can write well about clinical and professional developments for nursing magazines, as well as writing and editing textbooks and other nursing books. For you writers out there, there is also a need for nurses who can assist other nurses in preparing professional resumes. Some generalist professional resume writers—while meaning well—don't know the field as well as a nurse does, and cannot convey the depth and extent of a nurse's career the way a nurse can. And finally, for you budding consultants out there, two specialties are available, and they are both closely related to each other. The first is career consulting for nurses: working with nurses on strategies to advance their professional development as well as their lives. I would be remiss if I did not tell you that this is one of *my* specialties: the manual you are holding in your hand is a product of that type of work. But there's room for plenty more than me! Image consulting for nurses is another area that's growing: nurses who work with other nurses on their total "package": how to present themselves in a sometimes cutthroat professional field, and how to make what they know and what they *are* work best for them.

Nursing in Schools and Other "Child-Centered" Areas

There was a time—not so long ago—when it was thought that there were going to be nurses in every school in a few years, and that this was a golden opportunity for the advancement of nurses' careers. Well, like so many golden opportunities, it turned out to be more like a silver opportunity, but schools and other "child-centered" places is still a good place for nurses.

What earnest nurses failed to realize was that the budgets for schools would not grow as much as they thought they would, and it *is* expensive to have nurses in every school. But our point here is not to bemoan what could have been, but to help you deal with things as they are.

If you like working with children or adolescents, you are very possibly involved with them formally already. Perhaps you are working on a pediatric division of a hospital, or providing home care to children. What I would like to open your eyes to is the great many opportunities still available in schools.

There are not many nurses now working directly, one-on-one with a particular school, especially if the school is a garden variety school. Such nurses may find themselves working with several schools, dealing with a range of health concerns. There will be the usual public health type of issues—such things as lice infestations or hepatitis outbreaks. Increasingly, however, school nurses are working with health education, serving sometimes as teachers for various health classes, and sometimes for classes such as "health occupations," for students anticipating a health-oriented career. Sometimes they serve as consultants to teachers dealing with health education, especially in such areas as sex education, HIV education, and other STD's. In other words, the nurse who is in a school setting may be setting their own agendas, and carving out a new career path for nurses for the 21st century.

Nurses working in schools designed for the mentally or physically challenged will find themselves in a different and more intense situation. Such nurses will be intimately involved with the students' day-to-day functioning, and working with care and treatment plans in a group planning situation with teachers, administrators, physical therapists, mental health workers, physicians, and others involved with their care.

One area of working with children is seldom mentioned, but it is a worthwhile and—dare I say it?—fun area. That is camp nursing. I cannot imagine anyone being able to make a full-time career out of camp nursing (though doubtless someone has), but it can be an enjoyable way to be in a beautiful spot for several weeks every summer. I speak with some experience. I volunteer one week every summer at a church camp in the mountains near our home. The work is *not* difficult, but it is fun, and I was shamed into doing it several years ago when an older nurse in our church scolded me for not having volunteered. It turned out that they had almost had to cancel the camp's mentally handicapped week that year because no nurse was available. So I went. And one week out of the summer I am immersed with children, usually about one hundred of them, my own children usually among them. I am there for the cuts, for the stomachaches, and for the vague symptoms that usually turn out to be homesickness. The absolutely worst injury I have had yet was my own son's: he and another camper were playing capture-the-flag, they collided spectacularly, and produced a nice gash above his eye. While we were in the ER, and his cut was being sewn up, he bragged to the doctor that his sunglasses didn't break. I was so grateful that he had not been hurt worse that I resisted the temptation to kill him with my bare hands. If only the glasses *had* broken, his face probably would not have been cut! But such is life …

While I am a volunteer, there are many camps that pay. The pay is sometimes good, sometimes bad, but always negotiable. Even most of the camps that do not officially pay provide some small remuneration for your trouble. (My camp gives me $80 in cash to help cover my expenses for the trip up to camp). If you enjoy being with children, and enjoy becoming a tad younger for a week or more every year, consider this opportunity.

Money, however, in this case, is not the main reason I go every year. It is the satisfaction of seeing how much my own and other people's children enjoy the learning, the fun and the outdoors. I wouldn't miss it for the world. You will be a better nurse—not to mention the benefits the campers will receive—if you do it as well.

Traveling Nurses

If you're like me, and have the occasional bug for travel (or even a not-so-occasional bug) becoming a full or part-time traveling nurse may be right up your alley.

There are nurses who do not even have a permanent address, just a mail drop where they get their mail, because they are permanently working in different locations. Summers may find them in a cool spot, while they may winter in Los Angeles or Houston. There are other nurses who decide that they would like to vacation in a certain spot, and they would like the vacation to be a little longer than a week, so they sign up for a six week stint in Hawaii. There are any number of variations on this, and many nurses do any or all of them.

The basic premise is that there are areas where nurses are needed, so badly that hospitals and agencies are willing to pay your way to that location, as well as providing housing and often many other amenities as well. When you get to your location, you will be working for a hospital you've already agreed to, in a specialty you've already consented to. The number of specialties is often limited only by your imagination, and such agencies and some hospitals are frequent advertisers in all of the big nursing journals. I would suggest contacting a number of them, and find out what is the best deal for you and your situation. Agencies vary widely in quality and in their dedication to the nurses they employ, and it behooves you to ask. Some questions you will want to ask: what kind of housing is provided? will you be sharing housing with anyone? are there guarantees as to the length of your contract? whom at the agency will you be able to contact should the situation not be working out? will they provide transportation for your family? will you be able to cash a check somewhere if you don't have a bank account in the city where you're going?

And if you're even more adventuresome, there are plenty of overseas nursing opportunities as well. These are also advertised in the same journals, differing little from domestic opportunities, except that they frequently require a longer contract, often as much as two years. Other overseas opportunities include some non-profit organizations, and charitable groups. Remember that we are not simply stressing making a living in this manual. *I am helping you make a life.* There is a big difference. Some of these will be paid opportunities, and some will not, and there will be all kinds of variations in the compensation. And remember that compensation can come in non-monetary forms, as well. Operation Smile, for example, brings nurses and physicians into areas for short terms. I have not worked with them, but I would imagine that the look on the face of parents of a child whose cleft palate has been corrected would be a very great compensation. Decide what you want to do, and look around. Imagination is one of the human gifts most overlooked, and underused, and yet its active use will repay you a thousandfold.

There are also opportunities for nurses on cruise ships, and nurses are needed for medical evacuation flights. To find more information about these opportunities, contact the various cruise line companies, as well as agencies which advertise in the big nursing journals.

The big question about travel is that often you can combine your professional career with the chance to see the world. Travel can fulfill several needs: your career, monetary needs, love of adventure, and a chance to help others. Life is too short to do only one thing at a time. Whenever you can, let yourself combine several needs into one thing. Travel nursing can allow you to do that.

SALES AND NURSING

If the average person's greatest fear is speaking in front of a crowd, then the second greatest fear must be that of selling. Most of us grew up with the idea of selling as a slightly dishonest pushing of unwanted goods on people who dreaded the sight of the salesman. But it does not have to be so. And the big secret is that *all* of us are in selling, even if it is nothing more than selling *ourselves* when we are in a job interview. When we think of it that way, selling can seem a little less forbidding, and truth to tell, *sales can be fun.* I learned this the easy way. When I began practicing nursing on my own, one of the things I did was paramedical examinations for insurance companies. Although there was fairly fierce competition where I live, I somehow got the idea that it was better *not* to knock my competitors, but rather to offer myself. And I did that. I went to probably fifty insurance agents. When I went, I said hello, was generally friendly, and left a couple of business cards. I always stressed that while I knew my competition to be good (they were) I was also here, and ready to be of service. If one of my competitors was out of town, or for other reasons unable to take care of their needs, I would be happy to do so, and there would be no hard feelings if they went back to my competitor after using me that once.

It worked. First, in my ignorance, I somehow realized that knocking your competitor never works. People *assume* that you will not like your competitor, and they discount anything bad you might say about them. Secondly, no one likes hard sell. You don't, and neither do I. So don't hard sell. Play a little hard to get. Give off the air that you are terribly busy, but will be happy to squeeze them in. (Another rule: don't tell anyone that you are not busy, or that you are having a slow week, or whatever. This will *not* make them immediately feel like calling you; rather, they will wonder *why* you are not busy: Is there something wrong with your service? I am not telling you to lie, but please be a tad quiet about talking about how busy you are. You will also find that the busier you become, the more job offers you will have come to you. I am completely self-employed, and have no interest in becoming someone's employee, but I regularly get job offers. You will find the same thing happening to you).

But in this section, I am not primarily talking about selling your services, but about selling as a nursing practice. Pharmaceutical sales are the idea that springs to mind, and it has been a good opportunity to a lot of nurses. But there are other choices available. And don't rule yourself out in sales right away. If you are friendly, talkative, and find it easy (and fun) to persuade others about things you believe in, consider sales, at least the possibility. True selling is a means of doing good to others, and helping them. Those who do well in sales (and that is not the least of considerations: sales people are among the highest paid in the world, depending on their product) are not manipulating people, but helping them, and helping them a lot. There are many glib talkers who can sale through a sales presentation, and win a grudging sale from their target. But such people will seldom get a second sale, at least not from the same person.

I can only think of the man who has sold my family a fair amount of insurance. I have had health insurance with this man since 1982, and life insurance for several years as well. Never has he contacted me. Every time I have bought something, it has been my doing, and I have never once felt pressured by him. And yet I am rather constantly giving this man's name to others, and he has helped many of *them*, too. He has done very well for himself, judging from all external appearances. And yet he has stayed in that industry for many years, far outlasting the Roman candle-types who berate and nag their friends and relatives, and who seem to do very well…for a very short time.

Some of the sales-type areas to consider: health and medical product sales (whether to the public, to other nurses and health professionals, or to institutions such as hospitals), service sales (an example of this would be selling a specialized health promotion to various industries for hospitals), and network/multi-level health product sales.

A LITTLE MORE SEARCHING: THE INTERNET AND ALL THAT

Finally, I would be remiss if I didn't mention a large source of information for and about your nursing career: the internet. While the internet's great information bazaar seems huge and daunting now, what is currently available is nothing compared to what you will see in five or ten years. If you are not currently on-line, and using the internet, you are cutting yourself off from a helpful and inexpensive source of information, not just for your career, but for your life.

Our internet server charges us around $20 a month for unlimited service. You will probably pay somewhere in the neighborhood of $10-$20 monthly, depending on the number of hours you are on-line. Already there are some providers giving free internet service, and I suspect this is the wave of the future. Keep on the lookout for such offers. But whatever you pay, consider it an essential cost of doing business. You will not regret your learning to effectively use the internet in your nursing career.

If you don't have a computer yet, start looking now. As I write this in the spring of 2000, machines with monitors and printers are available for less than $500. The machine I'm writing this on cost around $700 when I bought it the day after Thanksgiving, 1998. The machines currently available are far better and cheaper. I usually replace my computer every two years. What you buy now will be outdated in a year or two, but it will serve you very well in the meantime.

I'm not suggesting you become a computer geek; what I *am* telling you is that if you are afraid of computers this is the time to get over it, and learn to use them. If you are working in a hospital or clinic setting, you are probably already using computers to some degree. It is not difficult, and it is amazing how little damage you can do while learning. I know very little about computers, but I know how to use them, and I use them all the time, and I know people who can help me when I'm stymied. Buy a computer, start using it, and learn as you go.

After you are on in internet, you will quickly find that search engines are your best bets for information finding. Search engines search the net by using keywords you give it, and it finds web sites which have information about the words you entered. For instance, entering "nurses" will return thousands or web sites that have the word nurses somewhere on the site. But you can make this a great deal more productive by entering several key words (such as "nurses," "careers," etc.) and thereby narrowing down your search. If you are looking for very specific information (say, about "legal nurse consulting," or about a particular company) you will probably get very helpful information that is quite up to date. I have found AltaVista to be the best (www.altavista.com), but there are literally dozens of search engines available, and more coming on board every week.

I would be remiss if I did not plug another resource available on the internet: discussion lists (sometimes called "discussion groups" or other title). These are email lists for individuals sharing a common interest, and there are many devoted to nurses and nursing topics. Check the lists available at onelist.com or globelist.com, or do some searching on a search engine. One of the good things about such lists is that they are almost universally free, and subscribing and unsubscribing are easy, so if a list sounds even remotely interesting, sign on for a day or two, and see how you like it. If the discussion is not something you find interesting, just unsubscribe. Remember also, that you are a part of the discussion, and your thoughts, insights, and experiences will all help make the list more interesting, both to you and others. I moderate a list which you may find of interest, devoted to nurse-entrepreneurs which includes you, if you are seeking to make your nursing career better. For further information, check out http:// www.onelist.com/ community/ NurseEntrepreneurs. You can subscribe from that page, or by sending a request to NurseEntrepreneurs-subscribe@onelist.com. I also publish a monthly on-line newsletter which gives updated information on the material in this book. If you are interested, send me a note at huffmanjim@hotmail.com, and I can put you on our mailing list. Of course, your name and email address will be kept private, and not sold, given, or traded to anyone else. But nurses *can* help each other, and the internet is a good way to do just that.

And before we leave the internet, allow me to plug what I am hoping will be a one-stop shopping site for nurses who are interested in making their lives better: my web site devoted to nurses networking with other nurses, entitled—appropriately enough: www.networkfornurses.com.

Books & Other Resources

While the internet is a wonderful tool, there is still a vast amount of learning to be had by good, old-fashioned books. If you are not in the habit of reading, may I suggest you take the habit up. It will prove amazingly useful in your career, and may very well make you a better person. Consider this: can you give up 15 minutes a day to reading? Life is hectic for most people these days, juggling careers, family and friends, and a great deal more. But if you can devote just 15 minutes a day to quality reading, you will—in the course of a couple of years—have gone through the equivalent of another college degree. Most of us are far more ignorant than we realize, and one of the marks of a truly wise person is a recognition of the limits of one's own knowledge. Continuing education can be a good thing, but simple reading can bring you an astonishing amount of knowledge. Reading is one of the few devices for time travel available to the average individual: through it, I can study with and interact with men and women who lived and died long before I was born. Through reading, I can study with teachers and masters who live far from me, or who are inaccessible to me, for whatever reason.

Of course, knowing where to start is difficult. My advice is to begin where you are interested, and allow your interests to lead you. Your interests tell a great deal about yourself. Go to a good, general purpose library, and find the area where the books of your interest area are shelved, and start looking. If it has been a while since you've used a library, make the acquaintance of the librarian. Librarians are information specialists, and they are frequently under-appreciated, and often under-valued. Most of the ones I've dealt with were gratified to be able to help someone interested in learning. And as I've said before, be not afraid of dumb questions. The dumb questions are the unasked ones.

Librarians can often help you find a book which you are unable to locate in the library itself, and libraries are usually able to provide you with inter-library loans. Inter-library loans are for titles not found in the library where you are searching, but which are available elsewhere. These inter-library loans are sometimes free, but at the most, there may be a nominal—$1-2—fee for postage (for mailing the book from the other library to your library). Often, an obscure book, difficult to find, and out of print for years, can be obtained by this method. I've also used it for books that were very expensive, and I wasn't sure I wanted to buy.

More expensive, but wonderful as well are the big "mega-bookstores" which came into prominence in the 1990's and are still with us today. Block out an hour or two, and spend time looking. These places often have an amazing variety of books, and the staff—while probably not quite as knowledgeable as your librarian—can be astonishingly helpful.

Likewise with used bookstores. While there are nowhere nearly as many of these as there were even twenty years ago, they can be a gold-mine of finds. They are best in college towns, where the buying and selling of information if a growth industry, but good ones can be found in surprising places.

On-line booksellers can be very good. Amazon.com is the industry leader, but bn.com (Barnes and Noble) is also very good. When I know the title I'm looking for, the best prices can be had from dealpilot.com. Dealpilot represents a large number of booksellers, and will direct you to the best deal for the particular book you are buying.

When you find a book you enjoy, or are helped by, look for other titles by the same author. Often we like a book because we resonate—for whatever reason—with the author, and many times, we will appreciate other writings by the same person.

Here are some suggested beginnings. These are books which I've found helpful in my nursing career. I've made some annotations as to *why* they were helpful. Obviously, I don't agree with everything in every book here, but these authors will help you if you let them. I have deliberately *not* given publishing information, since that tends to be quickly out of date.

1. The book that got me thinking (years ago) about taming the time monster was Alan Lakein's *How to Get Control of Your Time and Your Life*. It remains a book I turn back to every few years, and I gain insights every time. He will help you do what you want to do with your life: isn't that what you want?

2. Once, when I had suffered business setbacks, and was feeling sorry for myself, I chanced upon Michael LeBoeuf's *The Perfect Business*, and it, too, changed my life. The subtitle is *How to Make a Million from Home With No Payroll, No Debts, No Employee Headaches, and No Sleepless Nights,* and he tells you exactly that. While making a million dollars is not a goal of mine, he helped me, and will help you in this business career we call nursing.

3. Marsha Sinetar's *Do What You Love, The Money Will Follow* was helpful to me in one of those slumps when I knew I was doing the right thing, but I wasn't making much money doing it! I also recommend her book *To Build the Life You Want, Create the Work You Love.*

4. Richard Bolles has two books helpful in figuring out what it is exactly that you want to do, and how to get to that wonderful place. His most famous is *What Color is Your Parachute?* (now updated on a regular basis) and equally useful, but less well-known *The Three Boxes of Life And How to Get Out of Them.*

5. Barbara Brabec's *Homemade Money* is exceptionally helpful in figuring out some of the nuts and bolts of a home-based business, which is where I presume you'll be starting.

6. Jay Conrad Levinson's *Earning Money Without a Job* is useful not because of the job specifics he gives, but because of the picture he paints of a life in which you control your career,

rather than your career controlling you.

7. Finally, *Never Too Late*, by John Holt. Nothing whatsoever about nursing or business, this book is rather the story of how Holt began seriously playing the cello after he was 40, and in that delicate time of life when most of us think an old dog can't learn new tricks. For those of you thinking you are too old to begin anew, find this book, and gain hope that you can indeed begin something new.

HERE'S WHERE IT ENDS

Are you still with me? Because the title I gave this section is not exactly correct. This is *not* the end. Winston Churchill put it better than I can. While speaking in the middle of World War II, he reminded his listeners that the time in which he spoke was not the end. It was not, he went on, even the beginning of the end. But it *was* the end of the beginning.

And so this. This is not the end of your search for a better, more reliable, and more enjoyable nursing career. It is probably not the beginning of the end, either. But it is—I hope—the end of the beginning. In a sense, a manual like this can never make an entrepreneur, an innovator, a visionary out of you. I know that. There is in many the love for change and making things happen, and I'm not sure what puts it there. If that dream is in you, you will recognize that thrill of excitement when you read these pages. So start dreaming. And even better, start putting the dreams into action.

Can you do everything you need to today? Definitely not. Can you start doing *something* today? Absolutely. So start that one thing, and make your life more of what you wanted it to be. And start now. There's no better time.

INDEX

adolescent, 45,
agency, 29, 38, 45, 59,
AIDS/HIV, 44
alcohol, 44-45,
architectural, 45,
auction, 34,
bargaining, 6,
birth, 45,
Bolles, Richard, 71
books, 2, 27, 46, 56, 69-71,
bookstores, 70,
Brabec, Barbara, 71
briefcase, 33-34, 43,
business, vii, 27, 30-33, 43-44, 47-48, 61, 65, 71-72,
business card, 31,
camp, 46, 57-58,
cancer, 44,
capital, 8, 27, 29, 44,
career, vi-vii, 10-11, 15, 18, 24, 27, 31, 38-39, 43, 46-47, 49, 52-53, 56-57, 60, 65, 67, 69-73,
child care, 46, 53,
children, ix, 2, 10, 14-16, 20, 53, 57-58,
Churchill, Winston, 73
clinic, 32, 66,
coaching, 45,
computer, 35, 45, 65-66,
consulting, vii, 44-45, 55-56, 66,
critical care, 22, 24, 29, 45, 51,
diabetes, 44,
dietary, 44,
discharge, 44, 51,

downsizing, 27,

dreams, 1-3, 6, 8-10, 13, 15-16, 18, 73,

eating, 2, 44,

education, 18, 40, 45, 51, 55, 57, 69,

elder, elderly,

emergency, 45,

equipment, 33-35, 43, 47,

evaluation, 15, 23,

exercises, 19, 21, 29,

factories, 21,

failure, 16-18,

free-lance, 28-29, 45, 48-49 56

generalist, 29, 51, 56,

geriatric, 22, 45,

goals, 2, 8-11, 13-15, 17-20,

handicapped, 46, 52, 54, 58,

Holt, John, 72

home, 16, 23-24, 29, 37-38, 45-48, 52-53, 57-58, 71,

home health, 29, 45-46, 48,

homeschooling, *

hospice, 44-46,

hospital, 1-2, 18, 23, 28, 32, 43, 45-47, 51-52, 54-55, 57, 59, 66,

ICF/ECF/extended care, 52

image, 33, 45, 56,

income streams, 27, 29,

industrial, 45,

infection, 45,

information, viii, 60, 65-67, 69-71,

inservice, 18, 45, 51, 55,

insurance, 45, 48, 52, 54, 61-62,

internet, 65-67, 69,

internship, 40

labor, 45,

Lakein, Alan, 71

lawyer, 41,

LeBoeuf, Michael,

legal, 45, 66,

Levinson, Jay Conrad, 71

librarians, 69-70,

lifetime question, 9, 14,

medical-surgical, 1, 46, 51,
mistakes, 2, 22-23, 41, 49,
money, 1-2, 5-6, 18, 27, 33, 41, 43, 48-49, 58, 71,
multi-level, 46, 63,
music, 5, 46,
neonatal, 45,
neurological, 45,
nurses,vii-viii, 22-23, 27-29, 31-32, 37, 39-41, 44-45, 47-49, 51-57, 59-60, 62-63, 66-67,
nursing, viii, 1, 3, 10, 13, 15, 18, 21-24, 28-29, 31, 38-39, 43-47, 49, 51-57, 59-62, 65-67, 70-73,
occupational, 44, 51,
office nursing, 46, 54,
oncology, 46,
opthamology,
orthopedic, 45,
ostomy, 44, 51, 54,
pain, 31, 41, 44, 51,
paramedical, 29, 45-46, 48, 53, 61,
pediatric, 45, 57,
pharmaceutical, 45, 62,
physician, 15, 55,
positioning, 27,
preceptorship,
private duty, 45, 48,
public health, 21, 46, 57,
pulmonary, 45,
reading, vii, 10, 22, 46, 69,
recruiting, 45, 56,
resumes, 45, 56,
sales, 31, 35, 45-46, 61-63,
school, vii, 1, 10, 13, 15, 18-19, 21, 45, 52, 56-57,
screening, 45-46,
search, 15, 34, 66, 73,
self-employment, 15, 29,
Sinetar, Marsha, 71,
smoking, 44,
solitude, 37,
specialty, 29, 33, 39-41, 44, 51, 54, 59,
sports, 23, 46,

television, 46,
transplant, 44,
travel, 2, 5, 7-8, 19, 46, 59-60, 69,
utilization, 44, 51,
workplace, 37,

www.ingramcontent.com/pod-product-compliance
Lightning Source LLC
Chambersburg PA
CBHW030850180526
45163CB00004B/1518